I0423872

In the Year 1977

by

Kerry Butters.

In the Year 1977.

Millennium:	2nd millennium
Centuries:	19th century – **20th century** – 21st century
Decades:	1940s 1950s 1960s – **1970s** – 1980s 1990s 2000s
Years:	1974 1975 1976 – **1977** – 1978 1979 1980

1977 (MCMLXXVII) was a common year starting on Saturday (dominical letter B) of the Gregorian calendar, the 1977th year of the Common Era (CE) and *Anno Domini* (AD) designations, the 977th year of the 2nd millennium, the 77th year of the 20th century, and the 8th year of the 1970s decade.

Contents

Events.

January

- January – The world's first all-in-one home computer (keyboard/screen/tape storage), the Commodore PET, is demonstrated at the Consumer Electronics Show in Chicago
- January 1 – The Australian state of Queensland abolishes the inheritance tax.
- January 3 – Apple Computer is incorporated.
- January 6 – Record company EMI drops the controversial United Kingdom punk rock group the Sex Pistols.
- January 8 – Three bombs explode in Moscow within 37 minutes, killing seven. The bombings are attributed to an Armenian separatist group.
- January 10
  - Mount Nyiragongo erupts in eastern Zaire (now the Democratic Republic of the Congo).
  - Ocean Park opens in Hong Kong.

January 10: Ocean Park, Hong Kong

- January 15 – Linjeflyg Flight 618 crashes into the Kälvesta area of Stockholm, killing all 22 on board.
- January 17
  - Gary Gilmore is executed by firing squad in Utah (the first execution after the reintroduction of the death penalty in the U.S.).
  - 49 marines from the USS *Trenton* and USS *Guam* perished in the waters of the Barcelona harbour
- January 18
  - Scientists identify a previously unknown bacterium as the cause of the mysterious Legionnaires' disease.
  - Australia's worst railway disaster at Granville, near Sydney, leaves 83 people dead.
  - SFR Yugoslavia Prime minister Džemal Bijedić, his wife and 6 others are killed in a plane crash in Bosnia and Herzegovina.
- January 19
  - U.S. President Gerald Ford pardons Iva Toguri D'Aquino (aka "Tokyo Rose").
  - Snow falls in Miami (despite its ordinarily tropical climate) for the only time in its history. Snowfall has occurred farther south in the United States only on the high mountains of the state of Hawaii.

- January 20 – Jimmy Carter succeeds Gerald Ford as the 39th President of the United States.
- January 21 – U.S. President Jimmy Carter pardons Vietnam War draft evaders.
- January 23 – Prime Minister Indira Gandhi of India calls for fresh elections to the Lok Sabha and releases all political prisoners.
- January 23 – *Roots* begins its phenomenally successful run on ABC.
- January 24 – The Massacre of Atocha occurs during the Spanish transition to democracy.
- January 26 – Katimavik is founded as a volunteer service organization for Canadian youths.
- January 28 – The Great Lakes Blizzard of 1977 hits Buffalo, New York, and the Niagara Region of Southern Ontario.
- January 31 – The Centre Georges Pompidou is officially opened by French President Valéry Giscard d'Estaing.

February

- February 2 – The Congress party of India, led by Indira Gandhi, splits with Jagjivan Ram and other senior leaders, forming Congress for Democracy. This party later merges with the Janata Party.
- February 4 – Fleetwood Mac's Grammy-winning album *Rumours* is released.
- February 7
  - The Soviet Union launches *Soyuz 24* (Viktor Gorbatko, Yury Glazkov) to dock with the *Salyut 5* space station.

- London's *International Times* proclaims for the first time the famous quote; "punk is dead."
- February 15 – Space Shuttle program: First test taxi flight of Space Shuttle Enterprise.
  - The first Aardman character, Morph is introduced on Take Hart.
- February 18 – Prog 1 of 2000 AD is launched (issue dated 26 February 1977).
- February 23 – Óscar Romero becomes Archbishop of San Salvador.
- February 28 – Queen Elizabeth II opens the Parliament of New Zealand.

March

- March 4 – The 1977 Vrancea earthquake kills 1,500.
- March 5 – Formula One driver Tom Pryce dies after colliding with a track marshal at the South African Grand Prix in Kyalami.
- March 8 – The Australian parliament is opened by Elizabeth II, Queen of Australia.
- March 9 – Hanafi Siege: Approximately a dozen armed Hanafi Movement members take over 3 buildings in Washington, D.C., killing 1 person and taking more than 130 hostages (the hostage situation ends 2 days later).
- March 10 – The rings of Uranus are discovered.
- March 12 – The Centenary Test between Australia and England begins at the Melbourne Cricket Ground.
- March 15 – Tenor Luciano Pavarotti and the PBS opera series *Live from the Met* both make their American television

debuts. Pavarotti stars in a complete production of Puccini's *La Boheme*.

- March 19 – Results of elections to the Indian Parliament are declared. Indira Gandhi's Congress Party is routed by the opposition parties later to form the Janata Party.
- March 26 – Focus on the Family is founded by Dr. James Dobson.
- March 27 – Tenerife disaster: A collision between KLM and Pan Am Boeing 747s at Tenerife, Canary Islands, kills 583 people. This becomes the deadliest accident in aviation history.
- March 28 – Marquette University wins the men's NCAA basketball tournament with a win over the University of North Carolina 67-59.

April

- April 1 – The small market town of Hay-on-Wye declares independence from the UK, as a publicity stunt.
- April 2 – Horse racing: Red Rum wins a record third Grand National at Aintree Racecourse.
- April 4
  - Grundy, Virginia experiences a major flood that causes around $15 million in damages to 228 residential and commercial structures (to date the town is still recovering).
  - Southern Airways Flight 242 crashes on a highway in New Hope, Georgia, killing 72 people.

- April 7
  - German Federal Prosecutor Siegfried Buback and his driver are shot by 2 Red Army Faction members while waiting at a red light near his home in Karlsruhe. The "Ulrike Meinhof Commando" later claims responsibility.
  - The Toronto Blue Jays play their first game of baseball against the Chicago White Sox.
  - The Seattle Mariners play their first-ever game of baseball against the California Angels.

April 11: UK Silver Jubilee (25 red buses painted silver).

- April 8 – The punk band The Clash's debut album *The Clash* is released in the UK on CBS Records.
- April 11 – London Transport's Silver Jubilee buses are launched.
- April 21 – Residents of Dover, Massachusetts report sightings of an eerie monster.
- April 22 – Optical fiber is first used to carry live telephone traffic.
- April 27 – The Guatemala City air disaster kills 28 people.
- April 28 – A federal court in Stuttgart sentences Red Army Faction members Andreas Baader, Gudrun Ensslin, and Jan-Carl Raspe to life imprisonment.
- April 30 – The Cold War between Cambodia and Vietnam evolves into the Cambodian–Vietnamese War.
  - Led Zeppelin sets a new world record attendance for an indoor solo attraction at the Pontiac Silverdome when

76,229 persons attend a concert here on the group's 1977 North American Tour.

May

- May 1 – The Taksim Square massacre in Istanbul results in 34 deaths, hundreds of injuries.
- May 3 – The light aircraft carrier *HMS Invincible* is launched at Barrow-in-Furness by Elizabeth II.
- May 8 – Suzanne Lacy's extended performance piece about rape, *Three Weeks in May* begins in Los Angeles and continues until May 24.
- May 12 – Portugal and Israel establish diplomatic relations.
- May 14
  - The 1977 IAS Cargo Boeing 707 airplane crash in Lusaka, Zambia kills all 6 on board.
  - In Milan, Italy, during a far-left demonstration, a hooded person shoots at the police, killing a policeman, Antonio Custra. The scene is photographed and the picture of the hooded man shooting in the middle of the street appears in many magazines around the world.
- May 17
  - The Likud Party, led by Menachem Begin, wins the national elections in Israel.
  - Elizabeth II commences her 1977 Silver Jubilee tour in Glasgow, Scotland.
- May 23
  - Scientists report using bacteria in a lab to make insulin via gene splicing.

- Moluccan terrorists take over a school in Bovensmilde, northern Netherlands (105 hostages), and a passenger train on the Bovensmilde–Assen route nearby (90 hostages) at the same time. On June 11, Dutch Royal Marines storm the train, and 6 terrorists and 2 hostages are killed.
- May 25 – George Lucas' *Star Wars* opens in cinemas and later becomes the historic highest grossing film for that time. It also makes sci-fi films very popular.
- May 26 – George Willig climbs the South Tower of the World Trade Center.
- May 27
  - Elizabeth II opens the new Air Terminal Building at the Edinburgh Airport.
  - The 1977 Aeroflot Ilyushin 62 airplane crash in Cuba kills 69 people.
  - Space Mountain opens at Disneyland and to this day remains as one of the park's most popular attractions.
  - A demonstration and coup attempt in Angola takes place. Afterward thousands were killed by the government and Cuban forces.
- May 28 – The Beverly Hills Supper Club in Southgate, Kentucky, is engulfed in fire; 165 are killed inside.
- May 29 – Indianapolis 500: A. J. Foyt becomes the first driver to win the race 4 times.

June

- June 5
  - A bloodless coup installs France-Albert René as President of the Seychelles.
  - The Portland Trail Blazers defeat the Philadelphia 76ers 109–107 to win the National Basketball Association finals four games to two. Bill Walton is selected as the MVP of the series.
- June 6 – 9 – Jubilee celebrations are held in the United Kingdom to celebrate 25 years of Elizabeth II's reign.
- June 7 – After campaigning by Anita Bryant and her anti-gay "Save Our Children" crusade, Miami-Dade County, Florida voters overwhelmingly vote to repeal the county's "gay rights" ordinance.
- June 10
  - The first Apple II series computers go on sale.
  - James Earl Ray escapes from the Brushy Mountain State Prison in Petros, Tennessee; he is recaptured on June 13.
- June 12 – The Supremes perform their final concert together at Drury Lane in London, England and then disband permanently.
- June 15 – Spain has its first democratic elections, after 41 years under the Franco regime.
- June 16 – The Oracle Corporation is incorporated in Redwood Shores, California as Software Development Laboratories (SDL) by Larry Ellison, Bob Miner, and Ed Oates.
- June 20

- The U.S. Supreme Court rules that the states are not required to spend Medicaid funds on elective abortions.
- Anglia Television broadcasts the fake documentary *Alternative 3*, which enters into the conspiracy theory canon.
- June 21 – Bülent Ecevit, of CHP forms the new government of Turkey (40th government since the founding of the Turkish republic, but fails to receive the vote of confidence).
- June 25
  - The 1977 Rugby League World Cup culminates in Australia's 13 – 12 victory over Great Britain at the Sydney Cricket Ground before about 24,450 spectators.
  - American Roy Sullivan is struck by lightning for the seventh time.
- June 26
  - Elvis Presley holds his last concert at Market Square Arena in Indianapolis.
  - Some 200,000 protesters march through the streets of San Francisco, protesting Anita Bryant's anti-gay remarks and the murder of Robert Hillsborough.
  - 16-year-old shop assistant Jayne Macdonald is murdered by the Yorkshire Ripper in Leeds, England.
- June 27 – Djibouti receives its independence from France.
- June 30
  - The Southeast Asia Treaty Organization is permanently disbanded.
  - The Women Marines are disbanded, and the women are integrated into regular Marine Corps.

- U.S. President Jimmy Carter announces the cancellation of the B-1 Bomber program (it is later revived by the Reagan Administration).

July

- July 1
  - CKO (a Canadian all news radio network, defunct since 1989) begins broadcasting.
  - The EAC is dissolved.
  - Wimbledon – Virginia Wade wins women's singles title in centenary year of the tournament – It was Wade's first and only Wimbledon title, third and final Grand Slam title overall. Wade remains the last British woman to win the singles title at Wimbledon.
- July 5 – General Muhammad Zia-ul-Haq overthrows Zulfikar Ali Bhutto, the first elected Prime Minister of Pakistan.
- July 13
  - Somalia declares war on Ethiopia, starting the Ethio-Somali War.
  - The New York City blackout of 1977 lasts for 25 hours, resulting in looting and other disorder.
- July 15 – Anti-drug campaigner Donald Mackay disappears near Griffith, New South Wales (presumed murdered).
- July 19–20 – Flooding in Johnstown, Pennsylvania, caused by massive rainfall, kills over 75 people and causes billions in damage.
- July 21–24 – The Libyan–Egyptian War, sparked by a Libyan raid on Sallum, begins.

- July 21 – Süleyman Demirel, of AP forms the new government of Turkey (41st government a three-party coalition, so-called second national front (Turkish: *Milliyetçi cephe*)).
- July 22 – The purged Chinese Communist leader Deng Xiaoping is restored to power 9 months after the "Gang of Four" was expelled from power in a coup d'état.
- July 24 – Led Zeppelin presents its last American concert in Oakland, California, at the Oakland-Alameda County Coliseum. A brawl erupts between Led Zeppelin's crew and the staff of the promoter Bill Graham, resulting in criminal assault charges for several members of the Led Zeppelin group including the drummer John Bonham.
- July 27 – The Soviet Politburo orders Boris Yeltsin to demolish the Ipatiev House, where Tsar Nicholas II of Russia and his family were shot in 1918. Yeltsin eventually calls this a barbarian act.
- July 28 – The first oil through the Trans-Alaska Pipeline System reaches Valdez, Alaska.
- July 30 – Left-wing German terrorists Susanne Albrecht, Brigitte Mohnhaupt and a third person assassinate Jürgen Ponto, chairman of the Dresdner Bank in Oberursel, West Germany.

August

August 16: Elvis Presley dies. His funeral in Memphis attracts 75,000 fans.

- August 3
  - United States Senate hearings on Project MKUltra are held.
  - The Tandy Corporation TRS-80 Model I computer is announced at a press conference.
- August 4 – U.S. President Jimmy Carter signs legislation creating the United States Department of Energy.
- August 7 – Mount Usu volcano in Japan erupts.
- August 9 – The military-controlled government of Uruguay announces that it will return the nation to civilian rule through general elections in 1981 for a President and Congress.
- August 10 – David Berkowitz is captured in Yonkers, New York, after over a year of murders in New York City as the Son of Sam.

- August 12 – The NASA Space Shuttle, named *Enterprise*, makes its first test free-flight from the back of a Boeing 747 Shuttle Carrier Aircraft.
- August 15
  - The Big Ear, a radio telescope operated by Ohio State University as part of the SETI project, receives a radio signal from deep space; the event is named the Wow! signal for a notation made by a volunteer on the project.
  - Herbert Kappler escapes from the Caelian Hill military hospital in Rome.
- August 16
  - Elvis Presley, the "king of rock and roll", dies in his home in Graceland at age 42. 75,000 fans line the streets of Memphis for his funeral.
  - Supertanker *Pierre Guillaumat* is launched at Saint-Nazaire; she is the all-time world's largest ship (by deadweight tonnage and length overall) at launch.
- August 17 – The Soviet icebreaker *Arktika* becomes the first surface ship to reach the North Pole.
- August 19 – Groucho Marx, comedic legend, star of stage and screen, dies of pneumonia at Cedars-Sinai Medical Center in Los Angeles, at the age of 86 (born 1890).
- August 20 – Voyager program: The United States launches the Voyager 2 spacecraft.
- August 26 – The National Assembly of Quebec passes the Charter of the French Language (Law 101, *La charte de la langue française*) making French the official language of the Canadian province of Quebec.

September

- September – Evangelical pastor Oral Roberts publishes plans to build the 'City of God Hospital' in Tulsa, Oklahoma. The towers are completed in 1981 for $120M ($299M, in 2012)
- September 3 – The Commodore PET computer is first sold.
- September 4 – The Golden Dragon massacre takes place in San Francisco.
- September 5
  - Voyager program: *Voyager 1* is launched after a brief delay.
  - German Autumn: Employers Association President Hanns Martin Schleyer is kidnapped in Cologne, West Germany. The kidnappers kill 3 escorting police officers and his chauffeur. They demand the release of Red Army Faction prisoners.
- September 7 – Treaties between Panama and the United States on the status of the Panama Canal are signed. The U.S. agrees to transfer control of the canal to Panama at the end of the 20th century.
- September 8 – Interpol issues a resolution against the copyright infringement of video tapes and other material, which is still cited in warnings on opening pre-credits of videocassettes and DVDs.
- September 10 – Hamida Djandoubi's is the last guillotine execution in France.
- September 11 – Atari, Inc. releases its Video Computer System in North America.
- September 12 – South African activist Steve Biko dies after suffering a massive head injury in police custody in Pretoria.

- September 16 – Glam rock pioneer Marc Bolan dies in a car crash in Barnes, London.
- September 18 – *Courageous* (U.S.), skippered by Ted Turner, sweeps the Australian challenger *Australia* in the 24th America's Cup yacht race.
- September 19
    - Under pressure from the Carter Administration, President of Nicaragua Anastasio Somoza Debayle lifts the state of siege in Nicaragua.
    - North Korean agents abduct Yutaka Kume from Noto Peninsula starting the North Korean abductions of Japanese citizens.
- September 20 – The Petrozavodsk phenomenon is observed in the Soviet Union and some northern European countries.
- September 21 – A nuclear non-proliferation pact is signed by 15 countries, including the United States and the Soviet Union.
- September 23 – Jazz-rock group Steely Dan releases their sixth studio album *Aja*; it becomes their highest charting album in the United States at No. 3 and goes on to sell over 5 million copies.
- September 28 – The Porsche 928 debuts at the Geneva Motor Show.
- September 29
    - Singer-songwriter Billy Joel releases his fifth studio album *The Stranger*; it becomes the first of several hit albums, spawning five hit singles, going 10x platinum in the US, and later ranking at No. 70 on the list of Rolling Stone's 500 Greatest Albums of All Time.

- The modern Food Stamp Program begins when the Food Stamp Act of 1977 is enacted.

October

- October 1
    - Energy Research and Development Administration combined with the Federal Energy Administration to form United States Department of Energy.
- October 7
    - The Soviet Union adopts its third Constitution after a prolonged campaign by Brezhnev Supporters to have it passed before the Supreme Soviet dissolves for the end of the parliamentary session.
    - Pelé plays his final professional football game as a member of the New York Cosmos.
- October 13 – German Autumn: Four Palestinians hijack Lufthansa Flight 181 to Somalia and demand the release of 11 Red Army Faction members.
- October 14
    - Anita Bryant is famously pied by four gay rights activists during a press conference in Des Moines, Iowa. This event results in her political fallout from anti-gay activism.
    - American singer and actor Bing Crosby, one of the most popular, far-reaching and influential entertainers of all time, dies after finishing 18 holes at La Moraleja Gold Course in Spain.

- October 17–18 – German Autumn: GSG 9 troopers storm the hijacked Lufthansa passenger plane in Mogadishu, Somalia; 3 of the 4 hijackers die.
- October 18
  - German Autumn: Red Army Faction members Andreas Baader, Jan-Carl Raspe and Gudrun Ensslin commit suicide in Stammheim prison; Irmgard Möller fails (their supporters still claim they were murdered). They are buried on October 27.
  - Elizabeth II, Queen of Canada, opens the third session of the 30th Canadian Parliament.
  - Reggie Jackson blasts 3 home runs to lead the New York Yankees to a World Series victory over the Los Angeles Dodgers.
- October 19 – German Autumn: Kidnapped industrialist Hanns Martin Schleyer is found murdered in Mulhouse, France.
- October 20 – Three members of the rock band Lynyrd Skynyrd die in a charter plane crash outside Gillsburg, Mississippi, 3 days after the release of their fifth studio album *Street Survivors*.
- October 21 – The European Patent Institute is founded.
- October 25 – Seychelles recognizes the Sahrawi Arab Democratic Republic (SADR).
- October 26
  - The last natural smallpox case is discovered in Merca district, Somalia. The WHO and the CDC consider this date the anniversary of the eradication of smallpox, the most spectacular success of vaccination and, by extension, of modern science.

- Space Shuttle program: Last test taxi flight of Space Shuttle *Enterprise*, over California.
- October 27 – British punk band Sex Pistols release *Never Mind the Bollocks, Here's the Sex Pistols* on the Virgin Records label. Despite refusal by major retailers in the UK to stock it, it debuts at number one on the UK Album Charts the week after its release.
- October 28
  - Hong Kong police forces attack the ICAC headquarters.
  - British rock band Queen release the album *News of the World*.

November

- November 1 – 2060 Chiron, first of the outer Solar System asteroids known as Centaurs, is discovered by Charlie Kowal.

November 19: Sadat meets Menachem Begin in Israel.

November 2 – The worst storm in Athens' modern history causes havoc across the Greek capital and kills 38 people.

- November 6 – The Kelly Barnes Dam, located above Toccoa Falls Bible College near Toccoa, Georgia fails, killing 39.
- November 8

- Greek archaeologist Manolis Andronikos discovers the tomb of Philip II of Macedon at Vergina.
- San Francisco elects City Supervisor Harvey Milk, the first openly gay elected official of any large city in the U.S.
- November 9 – Gen. Hugo Banzer, president of the military government of Bolivia, announces that the constitutional democracy will be restored in 1978 instead of 1980 as previously provided.
- November 10 – The Bee Gees release the soundtrack to *Saturday Night Fever*, which will go on to become the then best selling album of all time.
- November 19
  - Egyptian President Anwar Sadat becomes the first Arab leader to make an official visit to Israel, when he meets with Israeli Prime Minister Menachem Begin, seeking a permanent peace settlement.
  - TAP Portugal Flight 425 crashes at Madeira Airport, Funchal, Portugal, killing 131 and leaving 33 survivors.
- November 22
  - British Airways inaugurates regular London to New York City supersonic Concorde service.
  - The TCP/IP test succeeds, connecting 3 ARPANET nodes (of 111), in what eventually becomes the Internet protocol.
- November 30 – The International Fund for Agricultural Development (IFAD) is founded as a specialized agency of the United Nations.

December

- December – the Colombo Plan for Co-operative Economic and Social Development in Asia and the Pacific (CESDAP) is implemented.
- December 1
  - Lockheed's top-secret stealth aircraft project, designated *Have Blue* and precursor to the U.S. Lockheed F-117 Nighthawk, makes its first flight.
  - The first children's cable channel The Pinwheel Network (later known as Nickelodeon), is launched.
- December 4
  - Jean-Bédel Bokassa, president of the Central African Republic, crowns himself Emperor.
  - Malaysian Airline System Flight 653 is hijacked and crashes in Tanjung Kupang, Johor, Malaysia, killing all 100 passengers and crew on board.
- December 11 – after losing 26 games, the Tampa Bay Buccaneers of the US National Football League record their very first win; against the New Orleans Saints.
- December 13 – a chartered Douglas DC-3 aircraft carrying the University of Evansville basketball team to Nashville, Tennessee, crashes in rain and dense fog about 90 seconds after takeoff from Evansville Regional Airport; 29 people die in the crash, including 14 members of the team and head coach Bob Watson.
- December 16
  - Mikhail Baryshnikov's 1976 production of Tchaikovsky's beloved ballet *The Nutcracker* comes to CBS a year after premiering onstage at the Kennedy

Center. This adaptation will become the most popular television production of the work.

- o The movie *Saturday Night Fever* is released in theaters and becoming the biggest dancing movie of all time and launches the career of its star John Travolta and the Bee Gees who performed many songs on its soundtrack to superstardom.
- December 18 – SA de Transport Aérien Flight 730, an international charter service from Zurich to Funchal Airport (Madeira), hits the sea during a landing attempt. Many of the 36 who die drown, trapped inside the sinking aircraft. Twenty-one people survive with the help of rescuers and by swimming to the shore.
- December 20 – Djibouti and Vietnam join the United Nations.
- December 22 – A grain elevator explodes in Westwego, Louisiana, killing 36.
- December 25 – Charlie Chaplin, comedian and silent film actor dies in his sleep at his home at the Manoir de Ban in Vevey, Switzerland at the age of 88.

Date unknown

Enterprise flies atop Boeing 747 over U.S.

- Portugal's traditional naming conventions change such that children's surnames can come from either the mother or the father, not just from the father.
- The Soviet National Anthem's lyrics are returned after a 24-year period, with Joseph Stalin's name omitted.
- Mormon sex in chains case with the alleged abduction in England of a young Mormon missionary.
- The WAVES are disbanded; women integrated into the regular Navy.

Births

January

Axel

Orlando Bloom

Leigh Whannell

Jerry Trainor

- January 1
    - Axel, Argentine singer and songwriter
    - Craig Reucassel, Australian comedian
    - Donna Ares, Bosnian singer
- January 2
    - Gavin Mahon, English footballer
    - Aleš Píša, Czech ice hockey player
- January 3
    - Mayumi Iizuka, Japanese voice actress
    - A. J. Burnett, American baseball player
    - Jim Shearer, American VJ (MTV2 and VH1) and television personality

- January 4 – Tim Wheeler, Irish singer-songwriter and musician (Ash)
- January 7
  - John Gidding, American actor and architect
  - Dustin Diamond, American actor
- January 8 – Amber Benson, American actress
- January 11 – Anni Friesinger-Postma, German speed skater
- January 13 – Orlando Bloom, British actor
- January 14 – Ruco Chan, Hong Kong actor
- January 17 – Leigh Whannell, Australian actor and writer
- January 19 – Taliesin Jaffe, American voice actor and actor
- January 20 – Melody, Belgian singer
- January 21 – Jerry Trainor, American actor
- January 22 – Hidetoshi Nakata, Japanese footballer
- January 23 – Kamal Heer, Punjabi singer and musician
- January 24 – Johann Urb, American actor
- January 25
  - Hatem Trabelsi, Tunisian footballer
  - The-Dream, American singer
  - Christian Ingebrigtsen, Norwegian singer (A1)
- January 26 – Vince Carter, American basketball player
- January 27 – Jermaine Jackson, Jr., African-American actor
- January 28
  - Lyle Overbay, American baseball player
  - Daunte Culpepper, American football player
  - Joey Fatone, American musician ('N Sync)
- January 31
  - Mark Dutiaume, Canadian hockey player
  - Kerry Washington, American actress

February

Shakira

Barry Hall

Cyrine Abdelnour

Mike Shinoda

- February 2
  - Shakira, Colombian musician
  - Jessica Wahls, German pop singer
- February 4 – Gavin DeGraw, singer/songwriter
- February 5
  - Adam Everett, American baseball player
  - Ahmad Merritt, American football player
  - Ben Ainslie, British sailor
- February 7 – Paul Comrie, Canadian ice hockey player
- February 8
  - Yucef Merhi, Venezuelan artist
  - Barry Hall, Australian rules footballer
- February 9 – Ledina Çelo, Albanian singer and model
- February 11
  - Randy Moss, American football player
  - Mike Shinoda, American rock musician (Linkin Park)
- February 16 – Ian Clarke, Irish computer scientist
- February 18
  - Ike Barinholtz, American actor, comedian and screenwriter

- László Nemes, Hungarian film director and screenwriter
- February 19 – Gianluca Zambrotta, Italian footballer
- February 20
  - Stephon Marbury, American basketball player
  - Amal Hijazi, Lebanese singer and model
- February 21
  - Cyrine Abdelnour, Lebanese singer, actress, and model
  - Jonathan Safran Foer, American author
  - Kevin Rose, American television host
- February 23 – Kristina Šmigun-Vähi, Estonian skier
- February 24
  - Floyd Mayweather Jr., boxing champion
  - Jason Akermanis, Australian rules footballer
- February 27 – Ji Sung, South Korean actor
- February 28
  - Jason Aldean, American country music singer
  - Rafael Amaya, Mexican model, singer, and actor

March

Chris Martin

James Van Der Beek

Jessica Chastain

- March 1 – Rens Blom, Dutch athlete
- March 2
  - Chris Martin, British rock musician (Coldplay)
  - Heather McComb, American actress
- March 3 – Ronan Keating, Irish singer (Boyzone)
- March 4
  - Ana Guevara, Mexican track and field athlete
  - Daniel Klewer, German footballer
  - Christian Jessen, TV presenter/doctor *Embarrassing Bodies*
- March 5 – Wally Szczerbiak, Spanish-born basketball player
- March 6
  - Paquillo Fernández, Spanish race walker

- Santino Marella, Canadian wrestler
- March 7
  - Ronan O'Gara, Irish rugby player
  - Mitja Zastrow, German-born swimmer
  - Paul Cattermole, English singer (S Club 7)
- March 8 – James Van Der Beek, American actor
- March 9 – Lydia Mackay, American voice actress
- March 10
  - Peter Enckelman, Finnish footballer
  - Shannon Miller, American gymnast
  - Rita Simons, English Actor
  - Robin Thicke, American-Canadian R&B singer-songwriter, musician, composer, and actor
- March 11
  - Becky Hammon, American basketball player
  - Jason Greeley, Canadian singer
- March 14 – Kim Nam-il, South Korean footballer
- March 15
  - Norifumi Yamamoto, Japanese mixed martial artist
  - Adrian Burnside, Australian baseball player
- March 16 – Ismael La Rosa, Peruvian actor
- March 18 – Zdeno Chára, Czechoslovakian (now Slovakia) hockey player
- March 23
  - Sammy Morris, American football player
  - Edwin Siu, Hong Kong actor and singer
- March 24
  - Jessica Chastain, American actress
  - Darren Lockyer, Australian rugby league player
- March 27

- Vítor Meira, Brazilian race car driver
- Roger Velasco, American actor

April

Michael Fassbender

Sarah Michelle Gellar

Frederik Magle

Arash

John Cena

Jason Earles

- April 1 – Vitor Belfort, Brazilian mixed martial artist
- April 2
    - Nicki Pedersen, Danish motorcycle rider
    - Michael Fassbender, German-Irish actor

- April 4 – Stephen Mulhern, British musician, TV presenter
- April 5 – Daniel Majstorović, Swedish soccer player
- April 9 – Gerard Way, American rock singer (My Chemical Romance)
- April 10 – Stephanie Sheh, American voice actress
- April 11 – DJ Fresh, English DJ, drum and bass and dubstep producer
- April 12
  - Tobias Angerer, German cross-country skier
  - Sarah Monahan, Australian actress
  - Sarah Jane Morris, American actress
- April 14
  - Sarah Michelle Gellar, American actress
  - Chandra Levy, American federal government intern (d. 2001)
  - Rob McElhenney, American actor
- April 15 – Dejan Milojevic, Serbian basketball player
- April 16
  - Fredrik Ljungberg, Swedish footballer
  - Tameka Empson, English actress
- April 17 – Frederik Magle, Danish composer, concert organist, and pianist
- April 21 – Jamie Salé, Canadian figure skater
- April 22
  - Anna Eriksson, Finnish pop-rock singer
  - Steven Price, British film composer
- April 23
  - Arash, Iranian-Swedish singer, entertainer and producer
  - Mariusz Pudzianowski, Polish strongman

- o Andruw Jones, Antillean baseball player
- o John Cena, American professional wrestler, actor and rapper
- o Kal Penn, American actor, producer and civil servant
- April 24
  - o Carlos Beltrán, Puerto Rican baseball player
  - o Siarhiej Bałachonaŭ, Belarusian writer
- April 25 – Manolo Cardona, Colombian actor
- April 26
  - o Jason Earles, American actor
  - o Tom Welling, American actor
- April 27 – Dai Fujikura, Japanese composer
- April 30
  - o Ole Jørn Myklebust, Norwegian Jazz musician
  - o Robert Evans, Welsh playwright

May

Ilse DeLange

Melanie Lynskey

- May 3
    - Ben Olsen, American footballer
    - Ryan Dempster, Canadian baseball player
    - Eric Church, American country music singer
- May 4 – Emily Perkins, Canadian actress
- May 5
    - Choi Kang-hee, South Korean actress
    - Virginie Efira, Belgian actress and television anchor
    - Jessica Schwarz, German film and TV actress
- May 8
    - Pepe Sánchez, Argentine basketball player
    - Chiaki Takahashi, Japanese voice actress
- May 9 – Choi Jung-yoon, South Korean actress
- May 10
    - Nick Heidfeld, German race car driver
    - Chas Licciardello, Australian comedian (*The Chaser*)
- May 11
    - Victor Matfield, South African rugby player
    - Janne Ahonen, Finnish ski jumper
- May 12
    - Graeme Dott, Scottish snooker player
    - Rebecca Herbst, American actress

- May 13
  - Ilse DeLange, Dutch country and pop singer, member of The Common Linnets, Eurovision Song Contest 2014 runner-up
  - Samantha Morton, British actress
- May 14
  - Roy Halladay, American baseball player
  - Ada Nicodemou, Australian actress
- May 16
  - Melanie Lynskey, New Zealand actress
  - Emilíana Torrini, Icelandic singer
- May 17 – Lisa Kelly, Irish singer
- May 19
  - Brandon Inge, American baseball player
  - Kelly Sheridan, Canadian voice actress
- May 20 – Chad Muska, American skateboarder
- May 23
  - Ilia Kulik, Russian figure skater
  - Yevgeny Rodionov, Russian soldier (d. 1996)
- May 24 – Tamarine Tanasugarn, Thai tennis player
- May 26
  - Misaki Ito, Japanese actress
  - Luca Toni, Italian footballer
- May 27
  - Abderrahmane Hammad, Algerian athlete
  - Tommie van der Leegte, Dutch soccer player
- May 28 – Elisabeth Hasselbeck, American talk show host
- May 29 – Massimo Ambrosini, Italian football player
- May 31
  - Phil Devey, Canadian baseball player

- Domenico Fioravanti, Italian swimmer
- Greg Leeb, Canadian ice hockey player
- Joachim Olsen, Danish athlete
- Eric Christian Olsen, American actor
- June Sarpong, British television presenter
- Moses Sichone, Zambian footballer
- Petr Tenkrát, Czech ice hockey player

June

Zachary Quinto

Kanye West

- June 1
  - Danielle Harris, American actress
  - Sarah Wayne Callies, American actress
  - Jónsi, Icelandic singer
- June 2 – Zachary Quinto, American actor
- June 3 – Travis Hafner, American baseball player

- June 4 – Jordan Bratman, American celebrity
- June 5 – Nourhanne, Lebanese singer
- June 7 – Marcin Baszczyński, Polish footballer
- June 8 – Kanye West, American rapper and record producer
- June 9 – Peja Stojaković, Serbian basketball player
- June 10
    - Adam Darski, Polish musician (aka Nergal, Holocausto)
    - Takako Matsu, Japanese singer-songwriter and actress
- June 11
    - Ryan Dunn, American television personality (d. 2011)
    - Geoff Ogilvy, Australian golfer
    - Shane Meier, Canadian actor
- June 12 – Ana Tijoux, French-Chilean musician
- June 14 – Chris McAlister, American football player
- June 16 – Kerry Wood, American baseball player
- June 19
    - Peter Warrick, American football player
    - Veronika Vařeková, Czech model
    - Maria Cioncan, distance runner from Romania (d. 2007)
- June 20 – Aaron Moule, Australian rugby league player
- June 21 – Jochen Hecht, German ice hockey player
- June 22 – Ryōko Ono, Japanese voice actress
- June 23
    - Antoine Winfield, American football player
    - Jason Mraz, American singer/songwriter
- June 25 – Naoya Tsukahara, Japanese gymnast
- June 26
    - William Kipsang, Kenyan long-distance runner
    - Tite Kubo, Japanese manga artist who created BLEACH

- June 27
  - Raúl, Spanish footballer
  - Arkadiusz Radomski, Polish footballer
- June 28 – Harun Tekin, Turkish rock vocalist and guitarist (Mor ve Ötesi)
- June 29 – Zuleikha Robinson, British actress and singer

July

Jarome Iginla

Victoria, Crown Princess of Sweden

Jonathan Rhys Meyers

- July 1
  - Jarome Iginla, Canadian hockey player
  - Liv Tyler, American actress
  - Tom Frager, French-born singer and surfer
- July 2 – Ricardo Medina, Jr., American actor
- July 6 – Craig Handley, British film director
- July 8
  - Milo Ventimiglia, American actor
  - Wang Zhizhi, Chinese basketball player
- July 10 – Schapelle Corby, Australian convicted drug smuggler
- July 11 – Edward Moss, American impersonator
- July 12
  - Peter Schaefer, Canadian ice hockey player
  - Brock Lesnar, American professional wrestler
- July 13 – Kari Wahlgren, American voice actress
- July 14 – Victoria, Crown Princess of Sweden
- July 15 – Ray Toro, American rock guitarist (*My Chemical Romance*)
- July 18 – Alfian bin Sa'at, Singaporean writer, poet and playwright
- July 19 – Jean-Sébastien Aubin, Canadian ice hockey player
- July 21 – Paul Casey, English golfer
- July 24
  - Mehdi Mahdavikia, Iranian football player
  - Danny Dyer, English actor
- July 26 – Rebecca St. James, Australian-born Christian musician
- July 27
  - Jonathan Rhys Meyers, Irish actor

- o Martha Madison, American actress
- July 28
  - o Manu Ginóbili, Argentine basketball player
  - o Rahman "Rock" Harper, American personality, restauranteur
- July 30 – Jaime Pressly, American actress
- July 31 – Tim Couch, American football player

August

Edward Furlong

Tom Brady

- August 2 – Edward Furlong, American actor
- August 3 – Tom Brady, American football player
- August 7 – Twins Samantha Ronson and Charlotte Ronson, British DJ and designer
- August 8 – Marílson Gomes dos Santos, Brazilian long-distance runner

- August 9 – Chamique Holdsclaw, American basketball player
- August 10 – Danny Griffin, Irish footballer
- August 12
  - Plaxico Burress, African-American football player
  - Park Yong-ha, South Korean actor and singer (d. 2010)
- August 13
  - Michael Klim, Australian swimmer
  - Miho Konishi, Japanese actress
- August 15
  - Martin Biron, Canadian hockey player
  - Igor Cassina, Italian gymnast
  - Anthony Rocca, Australian rules footballer
- August 16 – Tamer Hosny, Egyptian singer/actor
- August 17
  - Thierry Henry, French footballer
  - Tarja Turunen, Finnish operatic soprano
  - Claire Richards, English singer (Steps)
- August 18 – Lukáš Bauer, Czech cross-country skier
- August 20
  - Felipe Contepomi, Argentine rugby player
  - Manuel Contepomi, Argentine rugby player
  - Henning Stensrud, Norwegian ski jumper
- August 22 – Miho Kanno, Japanese actress and singer
- August 23
  - Nicole Bobek, American figure skater
  - Kenta Miyake, Japanese voice actor
- August 24
  - Robert Enke, German footballer (d. 2009)
  - Per Gade, Danish footballer

- Jürgen Macho, Austrian footballer
- August 25 – Masumi Asano, Japanese voice actress
- August 26 – Morris Peterson, American basketball player
- August 27 – Deco, Portuguese footballer
- August 30
  - Shaun Alexander, American football player
  - Jens Ludwig, German guitarist
  - Kamil Kosowski, Polish footballer
  - Sayori Ishizuka, Japanese voice actress
- August 31
  - Jeff Hardy, American professional wrestler
  - Barry Winchell, infantry soldier in the United States Army (d. 1999)
  - Craig Nicholls, Australian rock musician and songwriter

September

Ludacris

Tom Hardy

- September 2
    - Frédéric Kanouté, Mali soccer player
    - Elitsa Todorova, Bulgarian singer-songwriter
- September 4
    - Ian Grushka, American bassist (New Found Glory)
    - Lucie Silvas, English singer
- September 6 – Kiyoshi Hikawa, Japanese enka singer
- September 11 – Ludacris, American rapper
- September 12 – Idan Raichel, Israeli singer-songwriter
- September 13 – Fiona Apple, American singer
- September 15
    - Angela Aki, Japanese singer-songwriter
    - Tom Hardy, English actor
    - Jason Terry, American basketball player
- September 18 – Kieran West, British Olympic oarsman
- September 19
    - Ryan Dusick, American musician (former Maroon 5)
    - Ioana Maria Lupașcu, Romanian pianist
- September 20 – Namie Amuro, Japanese singer
- September 21 – Hank Fraley, American football player
- September 22 – Paul Sculthorpe, English rugby league player

- September 23
  - Matthieu Descoteaux, Canadian ice hockey player
  - Suzanne Tamim, Lebanese singer, actress, and murder victim (d. 2008)
- September 24 – Kabeer Gbaja-Biamila, American football player
- September 25
  - Adam Lovell, founder and owner of WriteAPrisoner.com
  - Clea DuVall, American actress
- September 27 – Andrus Värnik, Estonian javelin thrower
- September 28
  - Ivana Božilović, Serbian model and actress
  - Se-Ri Pak, South Korean golfer
  - Kristal Tin, Hong Kong actress
- September 29 – Jorgito Vargas, Jr., Canadian actor
- September 30 – Roy Carroll, Irish footballer

October

Matt Bomer

Jon Heder

- October 5 – Hugleikur Dagsson, Icelandic artist
- October 6 – Daniel Brière, Canadian ice hockey player
- October 7
    - Meighan Desmond, New Zealand actress
    - Yukta Mookhey, former Miss World and Indian actress.
- October 8 – Anne-Caroline Chausson, French mountain bicycle racer
- October 9
    - Hicham Chami, Moroccan financier and musician
    - Yafeu Fula (aka Yaki Kadafi), rapper from Tupac Shakur's group The Outlawz (d. 1996)
- October 11
    - Claudia Palacios, Colombian journalist and newsreader
    - Rhett McLaughlin, American musician and internet personality, host of "Good Mythical Morning"
    - Matt Bomer, American film, stage, and television actor
- October 12 – Bode Miller, American skier
- October 13
    - Paul Pierce, American basketball player

- o Quincy Carter, American football Player
- October 14
    - o Adam Pengilly, British skeleton racer
    - o Bianca Beauchamp, Canadian latex model
    - o Kelly Schumacher, American basketball and volleyball player
- October 15 – David Sergio Trezeguet, French footballer
- October 16 – John Mayer, American musician and record producer
- October 17 – André Villas-Boas, Portuguese football manager
- October 18
    - o Ryan Nelsen, New Zealand footballer
    - o Paul Stalteri, Canadian footballer
- October 20 – Stewart Petrie Scottish actor
- October 25 – Birgit Prinz, German footballer
- October 26
    - o Jon Heder, American actor and screenwriter (*Napoleon Dynamite*)
    - o Louis Crayton, Swiss/Liberian footballer
- October 27 – Kumar Sangakkara, Sri Lankan cricketer
- October 28 – Jonas Rasmussen, Danish badminton player
- October 29 – Brendan Fehr, Canadian actor
- October 30 – Charmian Faulkner, missing Australian toddler

November

Maggie Gyllenhaal

Steve Aoki

- November 1 – Alistair Griffin, British singer and songwriter
- November 2 – Randy Harrison, American actor
- November 3 – Aria Giovanni, American model and actress
- November 4 – Larry Bigbie, American baseball player
- November 6
  - Patrícia Tavares, Portuguese actress
  - Dušan Kecman, Serbian basketball player
- November 8
  - João Rodrigo Silva Santos, Brazilian soccer player (d. 2013)
  - Bucky Covington, American country singer
  - Nick Punto, Italian-American baseball player
- November 10 – Brittany Murphy, American actress (d. 2009)

- November 13
  - Chanel Cole, New Zealand-born singer
  - Huang Xiaoming, Chinese actor and singer
- November 15 – Peter Phillips, son of Anne, Princess Royal and Captain Mark Phillips
- November 16
  - Oksana Baiul, Ukrainian figure skater
  - Maggie Gyllenhaal, American actress
- November 17 – Ryk Neethling, South African swimmer
- November 18 – Trent Barrett, Australian rugby league player
- November 19 – Kerri Strug, American gymnast
- November 20
  - Daniel Svensson, Swedish drummer
  - Josh Turner, American country music singer
- November 21 – Jonas Jennings, American football player
- November 22 – Michael Preston, English footballer
- November 23
  - Christopher Amott, Swedish musician
  - David Lucas, English footballer
- November 24 – Colin Hanks, American actor
- November 26 – Ivan Basso, Italian cyclist
- November 27 – Mika Tan, Asian-American adult film actress
- November 28 – DeMya Walker, American basketball player
- November 30 – Steve Aoki, American electro house DJ and founder of Dim Mak Records

December

Emmanuelle Chriqui

Psy

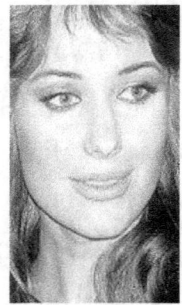

Oxana Fedorova

- December 3
  - Adam Małysz, Polish ski jumper
  - Troy Evans, American football player

- December 6
  - Andrew Flintoff, English cricketer
  - Paul McVeigh, Irish footballer
  - Miwa Yasuda, Japanese voice actress
- December 7
  - Fernando Vargas, American boxer
  - Luke Donald, English golfer
  - Dominic Howard Drummer in English rock-trio Muse
- December 8
  - Elsa Benítez, Mexican model and television host
  - Ryan Newman, American race car driver
  - Sébastien Chabal, French rugby union player
- December 10 – Emmanuelle Chriqui, Canadian actress
- December 11 – Peter Stringer, Irish rugby union player
- December 12
  - Dahm triplets, American models
  - Adam Saitiev, Chechen wrestler and Olympic gold medalist
- December 14
  - KaDee Strickland, American actress
  - Jamie Peacock, English rugby league player
- December 16
  - Kevin Gillespie, American comic book artist
  - Anu Nieminen, Finnish badminton player
- December 17
  - Oxana Fedorova, Russian personality, Miss Universe 2002 (dethroned)
  - Katheryn Winnick, Canadian actress
- December 20 – Sonja Aldén, Swedish pop singer

- December 21 – Gregor Horvatič, a Slovenian politician, former president of Slovenian Democratic Youth
- December 23
  - Alge Crumpler, American football player
  - Matt Baker, British television presenter
  - Jari Mäenpää, Finnish musician
- December 24 – Domingo Vega, also known as *Américo*, Chilean singer
- December 25 – Uhm Ji-won, South Korean actress
- December 27
  - Jacqueline Pillon, Canadian actress
  - Sam Talbot, American chef
- December 29
  - Laveranues Coles, American football player
  - Katherine Moennig, American actress
- December 30
  - Laila Ali, American boxer
  - Scott Lucas, Australian rules footballer
  - Kenyon Martin, American basketball player
  - Saša Ilić, Serbian football player
- December 31
  - Donald Trump, Jr., American executive vice-president of The Trump Organization
  - Psy, South Korean singer, songwriter, rapper, dancer, and record producer

Date unknown

- Hayko, Armenian singer
- Yaakov Shwekey, Jewish singer

Deaths

January

Anthony Eden

Carl Zuckmayer

- January 1
  - Adam Fox, Indian-born British male tennis player (b. 1883)
  - Michael Hogan (screenwriter), British screenwriter (b. 1893)
  - Johannes Pedersen (theologian), noted theologian and linguist (b. 1883)
- January 2 – Erroll Garner, American musician (b. 1921)
- January 3

- Carroll Quigley, American historian, polymath, and theorist of the evolution of civilizations (b. 1910)
- Hans Reinowski, German politician (b. 1900)
- January 5
  - Artur Adson, Estonian poet, writer and theatre critic (b. 1889)
  - Onslow Stevens, American actor (b. 1902)
- January 6 – William Gropper, American artist (b. 1897)
- January 11
  - Hilder F. Smith, pioneer aviator (b. 1890)
  - Henry Cronin, British civil engineer and army officer (b. 1894)
- January 12 – Henri-Georges Clouzot, French film director (b. 1907)
- January 13 – Henri Langlois, French film historian (b. 1914)
- January 14
  - Anthony Eden, Prime Minister of the United Kingdom (b. 1897)
  - Peter Finch, English-born actor (b. 1916)
  - Anaïs Nin, French author (b. 1903)
- January 16 – Daniel V. Gallery, American admiral and author (b. 1901)
- January 17 – Gary Gilmore, American murderer (executed) (b. 1940)
- January 18
  - Džemal Bijedić, Yugoslavian Prime Minister (b. 1917)
  - Carl Zuckmayer, German writer and playwright (b. 1896)
- January 19 – Yvonne Printemps, French singer and actress (b. 1895)

- January 21 – Sandro Penna, Italian poet (b. 1906)
- January 22 – Billy Down, English professional association footballer (b. 1898)
- January 23 – Toots Shor, New York restaurateur (b. 1903)
- January 24 – Eli Lilly (industrialist), pharmaceutical industrialist and philanthropist from Indianapolis,(b. 1885)
- January 27
  - Eero Nelimarkka, Finnish painter (b. 1891)
  - Walter Baldwin, prolific character actor (b. 1889)
- January 28 – Burt Mustin, American actor (b. 1884)
- January 29
  - Buster Nupen, South African cricketer (b. 1902)
  - Freddie Prinze, American actor and comedian (*Chico and the Man*) (b. 1954)

February

Louis Beel

- February 3 – Pauline Starke, American actress (b. 1901)
- February 4 – Brett Halliday, American writer (b. 1904)
- February 5 – Oskar Klein, Swedish theoretical physicist (b. 1894)
- February 6 – George John Park, New Zealand teacher and technical college principal (b. 1880)

- February 8 – Olinda Bozán, was an actress in Argentina (b. 1894)
- February 9 – Queen Alia, Queen of Jordan (b. 1948)
- February 11 – Fakhruddin Ali Ahmed, Indian lawyer and politician, 5th President of India (b, 1905)
  - Louis Beel, Dutch politician and jurist, Prime Minister of the Netherlands (1946–1948, 1958–1959) (b. 1902)
- February 12
  - Herman Dooyeweerd, Dutch juridical scholar by training (b. 1894)
  - Henry Jordan, American football player (Green Bay Packers) and a member of the Pro Football Hall of Fame (b. 1935)
- February 13 – Alberto Diena, Italy, was an expert on stamps of Italy (b. 1894)
- February 14 – Bill Tilman, English mountaineer and explorer(b. 1898)
- February 15 – Herman Johannes Lam, Dutch botanist (b. 1892)
- February 16
  - Rózsa Péter, Hungarian mathematician (b. 1905)
  - Carlos Pellicer, first wave of modernist Mexican poets (b. 1897)
- February 17 – Mary Anne Reidy, New Zealand civilian and military nurse, community leader (b. 1880)
- February 18
  - Andy Devine, American actor (b. 1905)
  - Ralph Graves, American actor (b. 1900)
- February 18 – Chandabai, Jain scholar and a pioneer of women's education in India(b. 1880)

- February 19 – Anthony Crosland, British author and politician (b. 1918)
- February 20
    - Ralph Hungerford, American naval officer, 33rd Governor of American Samoa (b. 1896)
    - Christoffel Venter, South African military commander (b. 1892)
    - Yisrael Alter, the fourth Rebbe of the Hasidic dynasty of Ger (b. 1895)
- February 21 – John Hubley, American animator (b. 1914)
- February 25
    - Patricia Haines, British actress (b. 1932)
    - Cuthbert Dukes, English physician and pathologist and author,(b. 1890)
- February 26 – Aurel Persu, Romanian engineer and pioneer car designer (b. 1890)
- February 27 – Allison Hayes, American actress (b. 1930)
- February 28 – Eddie "Rochester" Anderson, African-American actor (*The Jack Benny Show*) (b. 1905)

March

Willem Schermerhorn

- March 2 – Paul Rohmer, Alsacian physician considered the father of modern pædiatrics (b. 1876)
- March 3 – Percy Marmont, stage and screen actor (b. 1883)
- March 4
    - Andrés Caicedo, Colombian writer (b. 1951)
    - Ola Solberg, Norwegian newspaper editor and politician (b. 1886)
    - Lutz Graf Schwerin von Krosigk, German jurist and senior government official (b. 1887)
- March 5 – Tom Pryce, British Formula race car driver (b. 1949)
- March 8 – Henry Hull, American actor (b. 1890)
- March 10
    - E. Power Biggs, British-born American organist (b. 1906)
    - William G. James, Australian pianist and composer (b. 1892)
    - Léonce-Henri Burel, French cinematographer (b. 1892)
    - Willem Schermerhorn, Dutch politician and civil engineer, Prime Minister of the Netherlands (1945–1946) (b. 1894)
- March 11 – Ulysses S. Grant IV, American geologist and paleontologist (b. 1893)
- March 14
    - Black Mike Winage, Serbian-Canadian miner, pioneer (b. 1870)
    - Mae Carden, American educator who developed the Carden Method (b. 1894)
- March 15 – Antonino Rocca, professional wrestler (b. 1921)

- March 16 – Kamal Jumblatt, leader of the Lebanese Druze (b. 1917)
- March 17 – Claude Roger-Marx, French writer, and playwright (b. 1888)
- March 18 – Marien Ngouabi, President of The Republic of the Congo (assassinated) (b. 1938)
- March 19 – William L. Laurence, Jewish Lithuanian-born American journalist (b. 1888)
- March 22 – A. K. Gopalan, Indian communist leader (b. 1904)
- March 25
    - Nunnally Johnson, American screenwriter and director (b. 1897)
    - Joe Stydahar, American football player (Chicago Bears) and a member of the Pro Football Hall of Fame (b. 1912)
- March 26 – Madeleine Dring, British composer and actress (b. 1923)
- March 27 – Diana Hyland, American actress (b. 1936)
- March 28
    - Andries Mac Leod, Belgian-Swedish philosopher and mathematician (b. 1891)
    - Frithiof Nevanlinna, Finnish mathematician (b. 1894)
    - Marion Clyde McCarroll, writer and journalist (b. 1891)
- March 29
    - Charles Nicoletti, American gangster (b. 1916)
    - Eugen Wüster, industrialist and terminologist (b. 1898)
- March 30 – Abdel Halim Hafez, Egyptian singer and actor (b. 1929)
- March 31
    - Yasuji Kamada, Japanese photographer (b. 1883)

- Eric Grant Miles, served as an officer with the British Army (b. 1891)
- Jean Bachelet, French cinematographer (b. 1894)

April

- April 2 – He Tianjian, Chinese painter (b. 1891)
- April 2 – John Whitaker (gymnast), British gymnast (b. 1886)
- April 5 – Carlos Prío Socarrás, former President of Cuba (suicide) (b. 1903)
- April 6
  - Isaac B. Mitchell, American farmer and politician (b. 1888)
  - Frank Rooney, Austro-Hungarian Major League Baseball infielder (b. 1884)
- April 7 – Karl Ritter, German film producer and director (b. 1888)
- April 11 – Jacques Prévert, French poet and screenwriter (b. 1900)
- April 12 – Philip K. Wrigley, American chewing gum manufacturer and Major League Baseball executive (b. 1894)
- April 16 – Harwood Sturtevant, Episcopal bishop of the Diocese of Fond du Lac (b. 1888)
- April 17 – William Conway, Northern Irish cardinal (b. 1913)
- April 20
  - Wilmer Allison, American tennis champion (b. 1904)
  - Bryan Foy, American film producer and director (b. 1896)
- April 21 – Gummo Marx, American actor and comedian (b. 1892)

- April 23 – Charles D. Herron, general in the United States Army (b. 1877)
- April 26 – Jack Ayre, Canadian pianist (b. 1894)
- April 27 – Stanley Adams, American actor (b. 1915)
- April 28
  - Ricardo Cortez, American actor (b. 1899)
  - Sepp Herberger, German soccer coach (b. 1897)
  - Viktor Novak, Yugoslav historian of Croat descent (b. 1889)
- April 29 – William Arthur Whitlock, New Zealand journalist (b. 1891)

May

Ludwig Erhard

Joan Crawford

- May 4 – Richard Pike Bissell, author of short stories and novels (b. 1913)
- May 5
  - Ludwig Erhard, Chancellor of Germany (b. 1897)
  - Sam Lanin, American 1920s bandleader (b. 1891)
- May 9 – James Jones, American writer (b. 1921)
- May 10 – Joan Crawford, American actress
- May 13 – Otto Deßloch, German World War II Luftwaffe general (b. 1889)
  - May 15 –
  - Herbert Wilcox, British film director and producer (b. 1892)
  - Torsten Tegnér, Swedish athlete and journalist (b. 1888)
  - René Roy, French economist (b. 1894)
  - Yang Sen, Sichuan warlord and general who excelled himself in his long military career (b. 1884)
- May 16 – Modibo Keïta, former President of Mali (b. 1915)
- May 17 – Robert Maynard Hutchins,educational philosopher, dean of Yale Law School (b. 1899)
- May 18 – Czesław Wycech, Polish activist, politician and historian (b. 1899)
- May 25 – Máire Gill, political activist who became third and longest-serving president (b. 1891)
- May 31
  - William Castle, American film director (b. 1914)
  - Herbert Marshall (statistician), Canadian academic, statistician, and third Dominion Statistician (b. 1888)

June

Wernher von Braun

- June 2
  - Forrest Lewis, American actor (b. 1899)
  - Stephen Boyd, American film actor (*Fantastic Voyage*) (b. 1931)
- June 3
  - Archibald Hill, English physiologist, Nobel Prize laureate (b. 1886)
  - Roberto Rossellini, Italian film director (b. 1906)
- June 5 – Ward Melville,American philanthropist and businessman (b. 1887)
- June 9 – Walter B. Jones, American geologist and archaeologist (b. 1895)
- June 13 – Matthew Garber English child actor (b. 1956)
- June 14
  - Alan Reed, American actor (b. 1907)
  - Andy York, English professional footballer (b. 1894)
  - Leonard Barnes, British anti-colonialist writer, journalist and educationalist (b. 1895)

- June 16 – Wernher von Braun, German-born American rocket scientist (b. 1912)
- June 19
  - Geraldine Brooks, American actress (b. 1925)
  - Lady Olave Baden-Powell, English Chief Girl Guide (b. 1889)
  - Ali Shariati, Iranian sociologist (b. 1933)
- June 22
  - Jacqueline Audry, French film director (b. 1908)
  - Oscar Olstad, Norwegian gymnast (b. 1887)
  - Marston Morse, American mathematician (b. 1892)
  - Georges Miquelle, studies at the age of five (b. 1894)
  - Joan Evans, British historian (b. 1893)
  - Philip Lindsey Clark, English sculptor (b. 1889)
- June 25 – Olave Baden-Powell, founder of Scouting and Girl Guides, by over 35 years (b. 1889)

July

- July 2 – Vladimir Nabokov, Russian-born writer (*Lolita*) (b. 1899)
- July 9
  - Loren Eiseley, American anthropologist and writer (*The Immense Journey*) (b. 1907)
  - Alice Paul, American women's rights activist (b. 1885)
  - Harriette Chick, British protein scientist and nutritionist (b. 1875)
  - Willoughby Weaving, British writer and poet of the First World War era (b. 1885)
- July 13 – Carl Gustav von Rosen, Swedish pilot (b. 1909)

- July 15 – Konstantin Fedin, Russian writer (b. 1892)
- July 19 – Karl Ristikivi, Estonian writer (b. 1912)
- July 20
    - Carter DeHaven, American actor (b. 1886)
    - Grenfell Price, Australian geographer, historian and educationist (b. 1892)
- July 23 – Arsenio Erico, Paraguayan footballer (b. 1915)
- July 26 – Gena Branscombe, Canadian pianist, composer, music educator and choir conductor (b. 1881)
- July 30 – Jean de Laborde, French admiral, famous for the scuttling of the French fleet in Toulon (b. 1878)

August

Elvis Presley

Groucho Marx

- August 1 – Francis Gary Powers, American pilot, shot down in 1960 U-2 incident (b. 1929)
- August 3
  - Alfred Lunt, American actor (b. 1892)
  - Makarios III, Cypriot Archbishop and first President of Cyprus (b. 1913)
- August 4
  - Edgar Adrian, 1st Baron Adrian, English physiologist, Nobel Prize laureate (b. 1889)
  - Ernst Bloch, German Marxist philosopher (b. 1885)
  - Antonio Machín, Cuban singer (b. 1903)
- August 5 – Waldo L. Schmitt, American biologist (b. 1887)
- August 6 – Alexander Bustamante, 1st Prime Minister of Jamaica (b. 1884)
- August 9 – George Kenney, World War II United States Army Air Forces general (b. 1889)
- August 11 – John Howard Lawson, American screenwriter, one of the Hollywood Ten (b. 1894)
- August 13 – Henry Williamson, English naturalist, farmer and prolific ruralist (b. 1895)

- August 14
    - Ron Haydock, American actor, writer, and musician (b. 1940)
    - Alexander Luria, Soviet neuropsychologist (b. 1902)
- August 16 – Elvis Presley, American singer and actor (b. 1935)
- August 17 – Delmer Daves, American screenwriter and director (b. 1904)
- August 19
    - Groucho Marx, American actor and comedian (b. 1890)
    - John Harlow (director), English film director (b. 1896)
- August 22 – Sebastian Cabot, English actor (b. 1918)
- August 23 – Naum Gabo, prominent Russian sculptor (b. 1890)
- August 29 – Jean Hagen, American actress (b. 1923)
- August 31
    - Rick Vallin, Russian-American actor (b. 1919)
    - H. C. Potter, American film director (b. 1904)

September

Maria Callas

- September 1 – Ethel Waters, African-American singer (b. 1896)
- September 4 – E. F. Schumacher, British economist (b. 1911)
- September 6 – John Edensor Littlewood, British mathematician (b. 1885)
- September 8 – Zero Mostel, American film and stage actor (*A Funny Thing Happened on the Way to the Forum*) (b. 1915)
- September 9 – "Jungle" Jim Liberman, funny car drag racer (b. 1945)
- September 12
    - Steve Biko, South African activist (b. 1946)
    - Robert Lowell, American poet (b. 1917)
- September 13 – Leopold Stokowski, English conductor (b. 1882)
- September 16
    - Marc Bolan, English musician (b. 1947)
    - Maria Callas, American-born soprano (b. 1923)
    - Francis Shurrock, notable New Zealand sculptor and art teacher (b. 1887)
    - Alexandre Constantinovich Chnéour, Russian entomologist and herpetologist (b. 1884)
- September 18 – Paul Bernays, Swiss mathematician (b. 1888)
- September 23 – John Nash (artist), British painter of landscape and still-life (b. 1893)
- September 24
    - Piet Zwart, Dutch photographer, typographer, and industrial designer.(b. 1885)
    - Frederick Merk, American historian.(b. 1887)

- September 26 – Ernie Lombardi, American baseball player (Cincinnati Reds) and a member of the MLB Hall of Fame (b. 1908)
- September 27 – Czesław Wycech, Polish activist, politician and historian (b. 1899)
- September 28 – Adam Fox, Dean of Divinity at Magdalen College, Oxford (b. 1883)

October

Bing Crosby

- October 2 – Joseph William Woodrough, United States federal judge (b. 1873)
- October 3 – Tay Garnett, American film director (b. 1894)
- October 6 – Danny Greene, Irish American mobster killed by car bomb (b. 1933)
- October 8
  - Joe Greenstein, Polish-born American strongman (b. 1893)
  - Giorgos Papasideris, Greek country singer, composer, and lyricist (b. 1902)
  - Bucky Harris, Major League Baseball player (b. 1896)
- October 10
  - Helen Gibson, American actress (b. 1892)

- o Angelo Muscat, Maltese actor (b. 1930)
- October 12 – Dorothy Davenport, American actress (b. 1895)
- October 13 – Jackie Condon, American actor (b. 1918)
- October 14 – Bing Crosby, American singer and actor (b. 1903)
- October 16 – Cal Hubbard, American football player (Green Bay Packers) and a member of the Pro Football Hall of Fame (b. 1900)
- October 17 – Michael Balcon, English film producer (b. 1896)
- October 18 – Andreas Baader, West German member of Red Army Faction (b. 1943)
- October 20 – Members of the American southern rock group Lynyrd Skynyrd (killed in a plane crash):
    - o Cassie Gaines (b. 1948)
    - o Steve Gaines (b. 1949)
    - o Ronnie Van Zant (b. 1948)
- October 22 – Boye Schlytter, Norwegian businessperson and mountain climber (b. 1891)
- October 25 – Félix Gouin, French Socialist politician (b. 1884)
- October 27
    - o James M. Cain, American writer (b. 1892)
    - o Tony Hulman, American businessman and racetrack owner (b. 1901)
    - o Johannes Pedersen (theologian), theologian and linguist (b. 1883)
- October 30 – Frederick Hamilton March, Australian soldier and adventurer (b. 1891)

November

René Goscinny

- November 3 – Florence Vidor, American actress (b. 1895)
- November 4 – Betty Balfour, English screen actress (b. 1903)
- November 5
  - René Goscinny, French comic book writer (b. 1926)
  - Guy Lombardo, Canadian-American bandleader (b. 1902)
  - Alice May Palmer, New Zealand public servant (b. 1886)
- November 8 – Bucky Harris, American baseball manager (Washington Senators) and a member of the MLB Hall of Fame (b. 1896)
- November 9 – Gertrude Astor, American actress (b. 1887)
- November 10 – Dennis Wheatley, English writer (b. 1897)
- November 11
  - Greta Keller, Austrian-born singer and actress (b. 1903)

- Abraham Sarmiento, Jr., Filipino journalist and political activist (b. 1950)
- November 14
  - A. C. Bhaktivedanta Swami Prabhupada, Indian religious leader, founder-acharya of the International Society for Krishna Consciousness, ISKCON (b. 1896)
  - Ferdinand Heim, German general, branded the "Scapegoat of Stalingrad" (b. 1897)
- November 15 – Princess Charlotte of Monaco (b. 1898)
- November 16 – José Acosta (baseball), starting pitcher in Major League Baseball(b. 1891)
- November 17 – André Perugia, French shoe designer (b. 1893)
- November 18
  - Victor Francen, Belgian actor (b. 1888)
  - Kurt Schuschnigg, former Chancellor of Austria (b. 1897)
- November 21 – Richard Carlson, American actor (b. 1912)
- November 25 – Tommy Prince, Canadian war hero (b. 1915)
- November 28 – Claus von Wagner, German cabarettist and comedian
- November 30 – Terence Rattigan, English playwright (b. 1911)

December

Clementine Churchill

Charlie Chaplin

- December 3 – Jack Beresford, British Olympic rower (b. 1899)
- December 4 – Tom Senier, Irish melodeon (single row diatonic accordion) player (b. 1895)
- December 5
  - Rahsaan Roland Kirk, American jazz musician (b. 1936)
  - Katherine Milhous, American artist, illustrator, and writer (b. 1894)
  - Aleksandr Vasilevsky, Soviet general, Marshal of the Soviet Union (b. 1895)

- December 7 – Peter Carl Goldmark, Hungarian-born engineer and developer of the 33rpm record (b. 1906)
- December 10 – Ethel Roosevelt Derby, Youngest daughter of Theodore Roosevelt (b. 1891)
- December 12 – Clementine Churchill, Baroness Spencer-Churchill, Wife of Winston Churchill (b. 1885)
- December 13 – Sir Charles Petrie, British historian (b. 1895)
- December 15 – Wilfred Kitching, 7th (British) General of The Salvation Army (b. 1893)
- December 16
  - Gustaf Aulén, Bishop of Strängnäs in the Church of Sweden, (b. 1879)
  - Yngve Larsson, Swedish Ph.D., Municipal commissioner (Borgarråd), Member of Parliament and statesman., (b. 1881)
- December 18 – Cyril Ritchard, Australian actor and director (b. 1897)
- December 19
  - Takeo Kurita, Japanese admiral (b. 1889)
  - Jacques Tourneur, French director (b. 1904)
  - Nellie Tayloe Ross, American politician, the 14th Governor of Wyoming from 1925 to 1927 (b. 1876)
- December 24
  - Juan Velasco Alvarado, former military President of Peru (b. 1910)
  - Samael Aun Weor, Colombian writer (b. 1917)
- December 25
  - Sir Charles Chaplin, English-born comedian (b. 1889)
  - Oliver P. Smith, American general (b. 1893)

- December 26 – Howard Hawks, American film director (b. 1896)
- December 27 – Mildred Bendall, active force of the avant-garde in Bordeaux (b. 1891)
- December 28
    - Karen Grech, Maltese terrorism victim (b. 1962)
    - Charlotte Greenwood, American actress (b. 1890)

Date unknown

- Stephen Sanford, American heir and polo champion (b. 1899)

Nobel Prizes

- Physics – Philip Warren Anderson, Sir Nevill Francis Mott, John Hasbrouck Van Vleck
- Chemistry – Ilya Prigogine
- Physiology or Medicine – Roger Guillemin, Andrew Schally, Rosalyn Yalow
- Literature – Vicente Aleixandre
- Peace – Amnesty International
- Economics – Bertil Ohlin, James Meade

In the News.

The first Apple Computer goes on sale.

Jimmy Carter Elected President of United States.

Nobel Peace Prize is awarded to Amnesty International.

Jubilee celebrations are held 7th June in the United Kingdom to celebrate twenty-five years of Elizabeth II's reign.

World Trade Center in New York, is completed.

The last execution by guillotine in France.

Elvis Presley Dies from a heart attack aged 42.

Record company EMI sacks the controversial UK punk rock group the Sex Pistols.

Star Wars opens in cinemas and filmgoers line up for hours to see it.

Popular Films - Star Wars Episode IV: A New Hope, Rocky, Smokey and the Bandit, A Star Is Born, Saturday Night Fever, King Kong, Close Encounters of the Third Kind.

Voyager I and Voyager II are launched unmanned to explore the outer solar system.

The TV Mini Series "Roots" is aired on ABC winning top audience figures, 9 Emmys and a Golden Globe.

www.ingramcontent.com/pod-product-compliance
Lightning Source LLC
Chambersburg PA
CBHW071230280526
45787CB00002B/867